Unsolved Mysteries

Mysteries of the Ancients

Brian Innes

RSVP

**RAINTREE
STECK-VAUGHN**
PUBLISHERS
A Steck-Vaughn Company

Austin, Texas

Developed by Brown Partworks
Editor: Lindsey Lowe
Designer: Joan Curtis

Raintree Steck-Vaughn Publishers Staff
Project Manager: Joyce Spicer
Editor: Pam Wells

Library of Congress Cataloging-in-Publication Data
Innes, Brian.
    Mysteries of the ancients/by Brian Innes.
        p.   cm.—(Unsolved mysteries)
    Includes bibliographical references and index.
    Summary: Discusses unsolved mysteries left by ancient civilizations
including the stone figures on Easter Island, the city built by unknown
people on a Bolivian mountaintop, and the Great Pyramid of Khufu.
    ISBN 0-8172-5481-1 (Hardcover)
    ISBN 0-8172-4278-3 (Softcover)
    1. Civilization, Ancient—Juvenile literature. 2. Curiosities and
wonders—Juvenile literature. 3. Antiquities—Juvenile literature.
[1. Civilization, Ancient. 2. Curiosities and wonders. 3. Antiquities.]
I. Title. II. Series: Innes, Brian. Unsolved mysteries.
CB311.I54   1999
930—dc21   98-15505
                                                                CIP
                                                                AC

Printed and bound in the United States
1 2 3 4 5 6 7 8 9 0 WZ 02 01 00 99 98

Acknowledgments

Cover David Sutherland/Tony Stone Images;
Pages 5, 6, and 7: Wolfgang Kaehler/Corbis;
Page 8: James Amos/Corbis; **Page 10:** Kon-Tiki
Museum, Oslo, Norway; **Page 11:** Otto Lang/
Corbis; **Page 13:** Wolfgang Kaehler/Corbis;
Page 14: Mireille Vautier; **Pages 15 and 16:** Kevin
Schafer/Corbis; **Page 18:** Tony Morrison/South
American Pictures; **Page 20:** Galen Rowell/Corbis;
Page 21: Nik Wheeler/Corbis; **Page 23:** Roger
Ressmeyer/Corbis; **Pages 24 and 25:** Topham
Picturepoint; **Page 26:** Clive Druett/Papilio/Corbis;
Page 28: John Ross/Robert Harding Picture Library;
Page 30: Jonathan Blair/Corbis; **Page 31:** Jeremy
Horner/Corbis; **Page 33:** Gianni Dagli Orti/Corbis;
Pages 34 and 35: Charles & Josette Lenars/Corbis;
Page 37: Morton Beebe–S.F./Corbis; **Page 38:**
Hulton-Deutsch Collection/Corbis; **Page 41:** The
Purcell Team/Corbis; **Page 42:** Corbis-Bettmann;
Page 43: Owen Franken/Corbis; **Page 45:** Museo
del Oro Bogotá/ET Archive; **Page 46:** Tony
Morrison/South American Pictures.

Contents

Images in Stone

The mystery of the giant stone figures on Easter Island has puzzled people for centuries.

A tiny island lies in the rolling seas of the southern Pacific Ocean, some 2,000 miles (3,218 km) west of the coast of Chile, which is on the west coast of South America. The island is called Easter Island. The nearest populated land is Pitcairn, another tiny island, more than 1,000 miles (1,609 km) farther west.

Easter Island was given its name because a Dutch sailor, Jacob Roggeveen, first set eyes on it on Easter Sunday, 1722. When he went ashore, he was amazed to see hundreds of giant stone figures standing in rows along the cliffs. They were mounted on stone platforms that are called *ahu*. Some of these platforms had a single statue on top. Other platforms held as many as 15 figures. Each statue weighs as much as 50 tons. Some are as tall as 30 feet (9 m) high.

FINE CARVING

Stone figures gaze out to sea from the cliff tops of Easter Island (opposite). This was the sight that first greeted Jacob Roggeveen when he landed on the island in 1722.

The island is the remains of several ancient volcanoes. The figures have been carved from the soft volcanic stone. Some have a red hat, or crown, on their heads. This can be as much as 6 feet (1.8 m) high and 8 feet (2.5 m) wide. It is made from a different kind of volcanic stone and can weigh up to 16 tons alone.

"... he was amazed to see hundreds of giant stone figures standing in rows along the cliffs."

Most of the stone comes from the crater of a volcano called Rano Raraku, which is no longer active. This is at the northeast end of the island. Many unfinished statues were found there. The chisels used to carve them were still lying beside them. It appears that something had interrupted the work of the sculptors, and as a result of whatever this event was, they never went back to finish the statues.

UNSMILING FACES

All the figures have large, finely carved heads and round bodies. They have long faces with sharp jaws. Their noses are big, and their ears are long and narrow. All the figures have staring eyes and unsmiling mouths.

This Easter Island figure has a red hat. Could the red hat represent a man with red hair?

At the time of Jacob Roggeveen's visit, about 4,000 people were living on Easter Island. Strangely, although many of these people had the olive skin and dark hair typical of people from the Pacific Islands, others had blue eyes, reddish hair, and light-colored skin. When news of the island's discovery reached Europe, other people went there. However, not all of them went just to look at the statues. Some of the visitors were slave traders. They captured many of the people and took them away to be slaves all over the world. Tragically, by the mid–19th century fewer than 200 natives were left on the island.

At this time, the remaining islanders were introduced to Catholicism by Brother Eugène Eyraud. He was followed to the island by Father Roussel. Between 1883 and 1889, a U.S. Navy paymaster named W. J. Thompson visited Father Roussel. Thompson lived on the island for a time and made the first record of legends about the island's history.

STORIES FROM THE PAST

Some of the mysteries of Easter Island may have been carved onto wooden boards in what looks like a type of picture writing. These boards are called *rongo-rongo*, or "singing boards." Unfortunately, however, even the islanders that Thompson met during his visit did not know what they meant. To write his history, Thompson had to rely on local folklore, or stories passed down the generations by word of mouth.

This photograph of a group of children was taken on Easter Island in the present day.

The first visitors to Easter Island were puzzled. They found that many of the statues had been deliberately pushed facedown on the ground.

The natives told Thompson that the island was first settled by Pacific islanders, or Polynesians, who were led by their chief Hotu-matua. But they also spoke of an older people, the Hanau-Eepe, or "Long Ears." They said these were "very big men, but not giants." A later visitor was told that the first humans to live on the island were survivors of the world's first people. They were big, with long arms, broad chests, and huge ears. The visitor was also told that the first islanders had pure yellow hair and that they had come from a land that lay "behind America."

DEATH OF THE LONG EARS

One legend told how the "Long Ears" had been killed in huge numbers by people called the Hanau-Momoko, or "Short Ears." Only two Long Ears were spared. They became the ancestors of the light-skinned islanders of the present day. Experts worked out that the killing took place in about 1760. After this, many of the statues were knocked over.

For 200 years, archaeologists puzzled over how these statues had first been put up. There were no plants on the island from which strong cables could have been made to pull the statues up into place. Then, the Norwegian explorer Thor Heyerdahl made a scientific expedition to Easter Island in 1955.

KON-TIKI EXPEDITION

Heyerdahl was already famous for his southern Pacific voyage of 1947. He had wanted to show that people from South America could have sailed westward across the Pacific Ocean. He built a raft from balsa, which is a light, strong wood, and named it *Kon-Tiki*, or "the great god." Heyerdahl had left Peru and sailed more than 4,000 miles (6,436 km) in 101 days. He reached the tiny coral island of Raroia, east of Tahiti. His voyage had proved that, indeed, early peoples could have sailed across the waters of the Pacific Ocean on small rafts.

". . . the first humans to live on the island were survivors of the world's first people."

On Easter Island, Heyerdahl made friends with the mayor, Atan. This man was red-haired and claimed to be a Long Ear. He said the red crowns on the heads of some of the statues represented a topknot of red hair. Atan agreed to show Heyerdahl how a statue could be raised. Using three strong poles, a team of men lifted one a little way, then rested it on a pile of boulders. They pushed it up again and put

9

more boulders under it. To keep it from falling over, they held it in place with thin ropes until it was standing upright.

Atan told Heyerdahl that the statues probably stood on burial grounds, and that the statues were in memory of Long Ears who had died. But who were the Long Ears, and when did they come to Easter Island? Heyerdahl suggested that they had

In 1955, Thor Heyerdahl and a team of 12 men worked together. It took 18 days for them to raise one of the fallen 25-ton statues back onto its base.

arrived in about A.D. 380 and that they had come from Peru. However, in his book *Aku-Aku*, which describes his visit to the island, Heyerdahl wrote: "It was as if we had anchored with a hovering spaceship off the shore of an extinct world, where once had lived beings of a kind other than those on our Earth."

ALIENS FROM SPACE?

A Swiss hotel manager named Erich von Däniken seized upon this idea. In 1968 he wrote a book called *Chariots of the Gods?* This was a collection of so-called "facts" that von Däniken had distorted, or twisted, to fit his theories. He said aliens from space had visited Earth thousands of years ago. They were responsible for the huge ancient buildings all over the world.

About Easter Island, he wrote: "A maximum of 2,000 men was not nearly enough to carve these colossal [huge] figures out of the steel-hard volcanic stone, even if they worked day and night. . . . Then who did the work? . . . legend tells us that flying men landed and lit fires in ancient times." This is an example of the way von Däniken reasoned. But he was wrong on many counts. The volcanic stone is far from "steel-hard," and Atan had also shown Heyerdahl how it could have been carved. As for the "flying men," it is true that the Easter Islanders call their home the "land of the bird men." But this was because birds called terns came to the island to nest each spring. Men used to dive 900 feet (275 m) from a cliff into the sea in a contest to see who could be the first to seize an egg.

MYSTERY OF THE LONG EARS

Despite Thor Heyerdahl's discoveries, much of the mystery of Easter Island remains. Perhaps the Long Ears had come from Peru. But who were these fair-skinned, red-haired, people? The Toltecs, who lived in Mexico more than 1,000 years ago, also raised giant stone statues. Perhaps, one day soon, we may learn the true history of Easter Island.

This is an ancient Toltec temple in Mexico. Stone figures like those on Easter Island stand along the top. Could they have been built by the same people?

11

Ruins in the Clouds

Lake Titicaca (opposite) is high up in the Andes Mountains. The Andes run down the west side of South America, through Ecuador, Peru, Bolivia, and Chile.

Not far from the Bolivian capital of La Paz, in South America, are the ancient ruins of a once magnificent city called Tiahuanaco. The ruins stand high up in the Andes Mountains, at more than 12,500 feet (3,813 m). Close by is the great Lake Titicaca, which lies across the border between Bolivia and the neighboring country of Peru. This is a wild, lonely region. Yet it was here, high up in the clouds, that an unknown people built a great city of stone.

WHO BUILT THE CITY?

Francisco Pizarro was the first European to see Tiahuanaco. This was in 1532. Pizarro asked what sort of men had built the city. He was told that they were pale-skinned, bearded, and did not belong to the same race as the local natives. By the time Pizarro saw the city, it had been in ruins for many centuries, and little of what even he saw now remains. The Spanish invaders destroyed many of the buildings. Later, the local people used the great stone blocks from the buildings to build their villages.

Now, the remains of only two huge buildings, and two smaller ones, are left. The largest is the Akapana, also called "the fortress." It is

"This is a wild, lonely region. Yet here, high in the clouds, an unknown people built a great city of stone."

a natural mound that had been shaped and then covered with stones to create a great flat-topped pyramid. It is 700 feet (213 m) long, about 500 feet (152 m) wide, and 50 feet (15 m) high. The top covers 300,300 square feet (27,900 square meters). It was reached by a stone stairway.

GATEWAY OF THE SUN

The other great stone building is the temple, or Kalasasaya. It has huge pillars of stone that probably once supported a stone roof. Six enormous stone steps lead into the temple. The "Gateway of the Sun" is the most amazing feature of the temple. It is made from a single block of stone, 10 feet (3 m) long, 11 feet (3.5 m) high, and 3 feet (1 m) thick. It weighs nearly 10 tons. A busy scene is carved into the stone above the doorway. At its center is the figure of Viracocha, who was believed to have been the "creator of the world."

The magnificent carvings on the ancient Gateway of the Sun at Tiahuanaco. The central figure is said to be Viracocha. He holds a bow in one hand and two arrows in the other.

14

Huge steps lead up to one of the gateways into the temple at Tiahuanaco.
The statue of a man, some 12 feet (3.6 m) tall, is seen through the doorway.

There are 24 spear-carrying attendants on either side of Viracocha. Below the throne where he sits are 16 more figures. Originally, the carvings were colorful. They were covered with gold, and the eyes of the figures were made of jewels. These were all stolen many centuries ago. Nothing like this has been found anywhere else in South America.

GIGANTIC STATUES

Beside the temple stands a single statue of a man. It is about 12 feet (3.6 m) high. Because the figure appears to be holding a book, it has been called "the bishop." Cieza de Leon, an early visitor from Spain in about 1551, reported that he saw two more figures by the temple, each standing about 16 feet (5 m) high. He described them: "Two stone idols, of the human shape and figure, and the features very skillfully carved, so they appear to have been done

15

A stone wall at Tiahuanaco. The faces of several stone sculptures remain in place in the wall, although many have been badly worn away by the weather.

by the hand of some great master. They are so large that they seem like small giants. It is clear that they have a sort of clothing different from that now worn by the natives of these parts." This writer also described another great doorway that was similar to the Gateway of the Sun. He commented, "I fail to understand with what instruments or tools it might have been done."

MASTER BUILDERS

The other two remaining ruins are smaller than the Akapana and the Kalasasaya. These are the "palace," which is 196 feet (60 m) across, and the "Gateway of the Puma." Both ruins contain huge stone slabs as much as 37 feet (11 m) long and 15 feet (4.5 m) wide. Some weigh more than 100 tons. The stone has been carefully cut and grooved so that the slabs slot together. They are bound with copper clamps.

Tiahuanaco is now about 15 miles (24 km) from Lake Titicaca. However, the level of the water in the lake has dropped over the centuries. Once, the waters of the lake actually lapped at the foot of the city walls. About four hundred years ago, there were many more buildings to be seen.

LAKESIDE LIVING

A Spanish visitor in the 16th century described one building that stood beside the lake. There was a courtyard with walls two stories high. Along one side was a hall, about 45 feet (13 m) long and 22 feet (6.5 m) wide, "The roof of the hall, though it appears to be thatch, is really of stone. They have combed and carved the stone so that it resembles a roof of thatch. There are also many other stones carved into the shape of men and women, so naturally that they appear to be alive." He described how some figures were shown drinking from cups, while others sat, stood, or walked by a stream.

"I fail to understand with what instruments or tools it might have been done."

CIEZA DE LEON

According to these early visitors, the temples and palaces of Tiahuanaco were richly decorated with ornaments of gold and copper. On the walls, stone masks were hung from big gold nails. Most of these treasures were later stolen, but some have been recovered. The Posnansky Museum in La Paz holds some of the smaller statues and pots, as well as figures of humans, animals, and birds made of gold. There are also plates, cups, and spoons, and some of the golden nails that once held the masks.

This puma-headed vase was found in the ruins at Tiahuanaco.

The stones used to build the city of Tiahuanaco were from a volcanic region some 40 miles (65 km) away. But how could such huge blocks have been carried over such a long distance? And how were they worked with such primitive tools? Both questions have yet to be answered. Some archaeologists suggest that the city was built some time after A.D. 200. They say its civilization remained at the height of its powers for 500 years. But who were the people who built it?

LOCAL LEGENDS

One Spaniard who settled in the region in the 16th century was Juan de Betanzos. He married a young native woman and studied local legends. He was told: "In ancient times, the country of Peru was in darkness. . . . From a lake in this country, there came a chief called Kon Tiki Viracocha . . . . After he had sailed from this lake, he went to Tiahuanaco. He made the Sun and the day, and ordered the Sun to move in the course it now moves. And afterward, they say, he made the stars and the Moon."

All the descriptions of Viracocha agree on what he looked like. He was tall and pale-skinned. He wore a long white robe with a belt. His hair was short and shaved at the back, like a European priest. His name means "God, the Creator."

Juan de Betanzos was also told that: "In many places they tell how he [Virachocha] gave rules to men how they should live. He spoke lovingly to them with much kindness. He told them they should be good to each other and not do any harm or injury. Instead, they should love each other and show kindness. In many parts temples are built to him, in which they [the ancient peoples] placed stone statues in his likeness, in front of which they made sacrifices."

LOOKING FOR PROOF

These details must be treated with caution. The natives had already met Spanish priests, who were trying to teach them Christian beliefs. It is possible that they simply told the priests what they thought they wanted to hear. However, similar legends are found all over South America.

"From a lake in this country there came a chief called Kon Tiki Viracocha. . . ."

Because of the enormous size of the Tiahuanaco ruins, most Europeans could not believe that they had been built by the local people. They said that the Egyptians—or even a race of huge giants who had since vanished from the Earth—must have been responsible for the buildings. Some people believed in the story of the lost land of Atlantis, which had suddenly sunk beneath the sea. They claimed that these gigantic ruins were all that was left of this ancient civilization.

A POSSIBLE EXPLANATION?

There are several strange facts that could support this theory. There is a watermark, a line where water once met the land, that runs for over 300 miles (482 km) along the slopes of the mountains around Lake Titicaca. This watermark contains the fossil remains of seashore plants. Lake Titicaca is a saltwater lake. Some animals related to animals that live in the ocean are found in the lake. Also, the ruins of what looks like an ancient seaport were found close to the city of Tiahuanaco.

Some people suggest that the city once stood at sea level. Then, a massive movement of the Earth's crust forced the land nearly 2 miles (3 km) upward. But this would have taken thousands of years. It is unlikely that any buildings would have remained standing while this huge upheaval of the land took

Lake Titicaca as it looks today. Once, its waters would have covered the land up to the foot of the mountains in the distance.

People sailing reed boats on Lake Titicaca. This type of boat is cheap and easy to make from the natural materials found along the lakeside.

place. It would also have happened a very long time ago, yet many experts say that Tiahuanaco was built in around A.D. 200. That is a long time ago, but not long enough for the date to fit in with claims that the city of Atlantis was destroyed in about 10,000 B.C.

AN ANCIENT CONNECTION?

Those who believe the Egyptians built Tiahuanaco point to a strange connection. The reed boats that people still sail on Lake Titicaca are similar to those used in ancient Egypt. But the style of the carved figures at Tiahuanaco is very different from those in Egypt. Experts are confident there is no connection.

So the mystery remains. Where did the people who built the city of Tiahuanaco come from, and where did they go? How was the city built? And was the god Viracocha a real man?

21

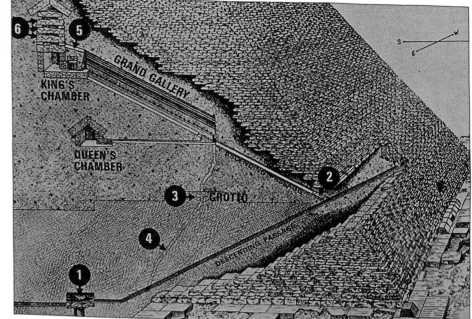

Diagram of the inside of the Great Pyramid, as discovered by the early explorers.
1. An empty chamber discovered at the end of the Descending Passage by Al Mamun.
2. The stone slabs that blocked the way to the Ascending Passage, the Grand Gallery, Queen's Chamber, and King's Chamber. **3.** The Grotto, which is as far as John Greaves went down a narrow shaft off the Ascending Passage in 1638. **4.** In 1764, Nathaniel Davison went farther down the shaft but found it blocked by rubble. **5.** Davison later found a small tunnel leading from the top of the Grand Gallery into a space above the King's Chamber.

pyramid. However, he could not find any hidden entrance, so his men stripped away the outer covering of stone slabs and dug straight through the huge stone blocks underneath.

Just as they were giving up hope of finding a way in, they broke into a narrow passage that sloped up and down. This is called the "Descending P...
When they climbed up, they found...
door that opened on the...
50 feet (15 m) ab...
downw...

Secrets of the Universe?

The secrets of Egypt's great pyramids may never be fully explained.

Some 10 miles (16 km) to the southwest of Cairo, Egypt, rises one of the Seven Wonders of the ancient world. This is the Great Pyramid of the pharaoh Khufu—the Greeks called him Cheops, and this name is still sometimes used. Its base covers 13 acres (5 hectares), and it is nearly 500 feet (152 m) tall. It was built from 2,300,000 limestone blocks. Each block measures 50 x 50 x 28 inches (127 x 127 x 71 cm) and weighs around 2.5 tons.

HOW WAS IT BUILT?

Experts cannot agree on how the pyramid was built. However, the most likely explanation is that a huge ramp of earth was piled up around the first blocks of stone. Then more blocks of stone were pushed on wooden rollers. Another possibility is that some kind of lifting equipment was used. When the pyramid was built, the outside of the pyramid was covered with...

A floodlit view of the Great Pyramid near Cairo, Egypt (opposite). Some claim the pyramid once contained the secrets of the universe. It is more likely th...

People sailing reed boats on Lake Titicaca. This type of boat is cheap and easy to make from the natural materials found along the lakeside.

place. It would also have happened a very long time ago, yet many experts say that Tiahuanaco was built in around A.D. 200. That is a long time ago, but not long enough for the date to fit in with claims that the city of Atlantis was destroyed in about 10,000 B.C.

AN ANCIENT CONNECTION?

Those who believe the Egyptians built Tiahuanaco point to a strange connection. The reed boats that people still sail on Lake Titicaca are similar to those used in ancient Egypt. But the style of the carved figures at Tiahuanaco is very different from those in Egypt. Experts are confident there is no connection.

So the mystery remains. Where did the people who built the city of Tiahuanaco come from, and where did they go? How was the city built? And was the god Viracocha a real man?

Secrets of the Universe?

The secrets of Egypt's great pyramids may never be fully explained.

A floodlit view of the Great Pyramid near Cairo, Egypt (opposite). Some claim the pyramid once contained the secrets of the universe. It is more likely that it was built as a tomb for pharaoh Khufu.

Some 10 miles (16 km) to the southwest of Cairo, Egypt, rises one of the Seven Wonders of the ancient world. This is the Great Pyramid of the pharaoh Khufu—the Greeks called him Cheops, and this name is still sometimes used. Its base covers 13 acres (5 hectares), and it is nearly 500 feet (152 m) tall. It was built from 2,300,000 limestone blocks. Each block measures 50 x 50 x 28 inches (127 x 127 x 71 cm) and weighs around 2.5 tons.

HOW WAS IT BUILT?

Experts cannot agree on how the pyramid was built. However, the most likely explanation is that a huge ramp of earth was piled up around the first blocks of stone. Then more blocks of stone were pushed up the ramp on wooden rollers. Another possibility is that some kind of lifting equipment was used. When it was newly built, the outside of the Great Pyramid was covered with smooth slabs of limestone.

In around A.D. 820, an Arab named Abdullah al Mamun took a gang of local workmen to see what was inside the pyramid. Al Mamun had been told there was a secret chamber in the

"... the four sides of the pyramid were accurately lined up with the four points of the compass. ..."

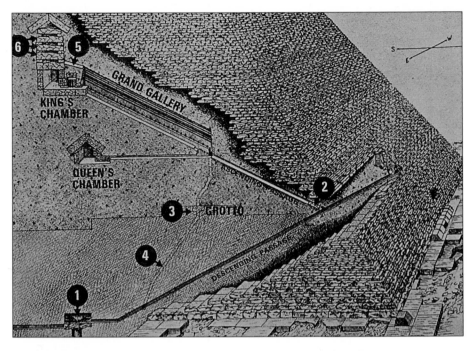

Diagram of the inside of the Great Pyramid, as discovered by the early explorers.
1. An empty chamber discovered at the end of the Descending Passage by Al Mamun.
2. The stone slabs that blocked the way to the Ascending Passage, the Grand Gallery, Queen's Chamber, and King's Chamber. **3.** The Grotto, which is as far as John Greaves went down a narrow shaft off the Ascending Passage in 1638. **4.** In 1764, Nathaniel Davison went farther down the shaft but found it blocked by rubble. **5.** Davison later found a small tunnel leading from the top of the Grand Gallery into a space above the King's Chamber.

pyramid. However, he could not find any hidden entrance, so his men stripped away the outer covering of stone slabs and dug straight through the huge stone blocks underneath.

Just as they were giving up hope of finding a way in, they broke into a narrow passage that sloped up and down. This is called the "Descending Passage." When they climbed up, they found a hinged stone door that opened on the north face of the pyramid, 50 feet (15 m) above the base. The same passage led downward to a small, empty chamber that had been dug in the rock below ground level. A horizontal passage ran another 50 feet (15 m) to a blank wall. From here, a narrow shaft went down another 30 feet (9 m) farther.

IN THE HEART OF THE PYRAMID

Then, Al Mamun and his men noticed a big block of granite wedged in the roof of the Descending Passage. It was heavy. They could not move it, so they had to cut around it. The stone was blocking a long, straight passage that sloped upward into the center of the pyramid. This is called the "Ascending Passage." It was blocked at several places by other large pieces of granite. They all appeared to have been wedged in from above. At the end of the Ascending Passage, a low, horizontal passageway led to a small, square room. This room is called the "Queen's Chamber."

Back where the horizontal passage began, the Arabs raised their oil lamps and, in the flickering light, saw an opening above their heads. Standing on one another's shoulders, they climbed into a huge corridor of smooth stone, 28 feet (8.5 m) high—the "Grand Gallery." This gallery sloped up at the same angle as the Ascending Passage. They were now at the exact center of the pyramid. There they found a horizontal

This painting shows what it might have been like inside the pyramid when Al Mamun and his men discovered the Grand Gallery.

passage, which led into a large chamber. This is now known as the "King's Chamber." At one end of the chamber was a huge granite coffin. It had no lid, and it was completely empty.

MYSTERY OF THE TOMB

Al Mamun had believed he would find ancient writings on astronomy hidden in the pyramid—perhaps even treasure. But there was nothing. The whole huge building was empty. He supposed that robbers had broken in and stolen everything. It seemed possible that the coffin had been made for the burial of the pharaoh Khufu. If so, then even his body had been carried off.

But there were no signs that anybody had ever broken into the King's Chamber. The granite blocks had not been removed from the Ascending Passage, and there was no other way out. Nevertheless, everybody still assumed that the Great Pyramid had been built as Khufu's tomb.

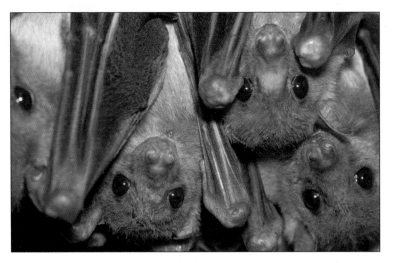

The only sign of life in the Great Pyramid was hundreds of bats. John Greaves was driven back by them in 1638, and they attacked Napoleon in 1798!

More than 800 years passed. Then, in 1638, the English mathematician John Greaves traveled to Egypt. He found the Descending Passage full of bats. At the top end of the Ascending Passage, where the Grand Gallery began, he discovered a narrow shaft going straight down into the darkness. He tried to explore how deep it went, but he was driven back by more bats. This shaft is actually 110 feet (33.5 m) deep. Back in England, Greaves produced a book of his survey, with diagrams.

"At one end of the chamber was a huge granite coffin. It had no lid, and it was empty."

In 1798, Napoleon Bonaparte was the leading general of France. That year, he led an army to invade and occupy Egypt. The army defeated the Egyptians at the bloody Battle of the Pyramids. Napoleon had taken a group of French scientists with him, and he ordered them to investigate the Great Pyramid. They tried to go inside but were attacked by thousands of bats. So they decided to make accurate measurements of the outside instead.

ANCIENT OBSERVATORY

The leader of the team was Edmé-François Jomard. He climbed to the top of the pyramid. There was a platform of 33 square feet (3 square meters) on top. Jomard worked out that the four sides of the pyramid were accurately lined up with the four points of the compass—north, south, east, and west.

This is the Grand Gallery. Handrails and lights have been put in along its length for the safety of the hundreds of tourists who visit the pyramid each year.

Jomard was sure that the Great Pyramid was an ancient system of measurements. He suspected that it had been built as an observatory. An astronomer, standing at the bottom of the Descending Passage and looking up, could time the movement of the stars as they circled around the North Star in the northern sky.

More than 80 years after Jomard's findings, an English astronomer, Richard Proctor, came across a piece of writing. This was a report that had been written by a Greek philosopher. His name was Proclus. In the report, Proclus said that the Great Pyramid had been used as an astronomical observatory before the building work was completed.

REFLECTIONS OF SPACE

This made good sense to Proctor, and he described how the observatory might have been built. First, the base of the pyramid was built up, until the entrance to the Descending Passage was on the outer face of the pyramid. At the same time, the Ascending Passage was made, pointing in the opposite direction, due south. Proctor suggested that a pool of water was kept at the point where the two passages began. An ancient astronomer could look down the pitch-dark Descending Passage and see light reflected, down the Ascending Passage, from stars in the southern sky. From here, he could measure the time as each star appeared in sight through the upper entrance of the Ascending Passage.

"Jomard was sure that the Great Pyramid was an ancient system of measurements."

Then, the Grand Gallery was built. It was like a giant slit. A vertical "slice" of the sky could be seen through it. Even though the height of the stars in the sky changes with the seasons, the astronomers would still have been able to see them clearly.

MEASURING THE EARTH

At this point in the building of the Great Pyramid, the Grand Gallery emerged onto a flat platform, at the level of the present King's Chamber. Proctor believed that this square was used for making an accurate map of the heavens.

More recently, Livio Stecchini, an American professor of the history of science, has claimed that the ancient Egyptians were able to make many discoveries from their studies of the movements of the Sun, Moon, and planets against the stars. They worked out the shape and size of Earth, the degrees of latitude and longitude, and measured the precise length of the year.

Stonehenge, on Salisbury Plain in Wiltshire, England. The huge circle of stones was probably built as an observatory. Shadows cast by the Sun and Moon show their movements across the sky.

If it were built as an observatory, the pyramid had to be large so that the ancient astronomers could make accurate measurements. This was, after all, about 4,000 years before the invention of the telescope. Other ancient observatories are also quite large. At Stonehenge, in England, huge stones weighing many tons have been arranged in a circle. These stones were used to plot the movements of the Sun and Moon. In India, at the cities of Delhi and Benares, there are the remains of other big stone observatories.

HIDDEN SECRETS

But why was the pyramid later completed? Some experts have suggested that when the astronomers had discovered all they wanted to know, they walled up their observatory so that nobody else could learn their methods. This would explain the legend that the Great Pyramid contained the secrets of the universe. It would also explain how the granite blocks were set in the Ascending Passage. As the top layers of the pyramid were being completed, the blocks were lowered into place from above. Some writers have also suggested that the astronomers told pharaoh Khufu that he could have the pyramid as his tomb. But it was a promise they did not intend to keep.

THE LOST PHARAOH

Many experts, however, do not believe the pyramid was ever used as an observatory. They are sure it was built for Khufu's tomb. They believe that there are other chambers still to be found, with the body of the pharaoh in one of them. And they hope that, one day, they will discover treasures even more splendid than those found in the tomb of Tutankhamen.

A view from one of the windows at the ancient Jantar Matar observatory, Delhi, India. This huge sundial shows the time of day from the position of the Sun.

31

Powers of the Pyramid

People who studied the Great Pyramid in Egypt claimed that it had amazing powers.

The discoveries of the passages and chambers inside Egypt's Great Pyramid near Cairo caused great world excitement. A wave of interest in ancient Egypt swept through Europe. In the 1860s, an English magazine editor named John Taylor was fascinated by the pyramid. He never visited Egypt. Instead, he built himself a model of the pyramid and studied it. To his amazement, Taylor found that if he took the length of two sides added together, then divided this by the height, he got a figure close to the value of pi (π). Pi is the constant figure that allows you to work out the circumference, or length around the outer edge, of any circle if you already know the diameter, or width.

Anything to do with the art and culture of ancient Egypt became the fashion in 19th-century Europe. This French print from the period (opposite) shows an artist's idea of the inside of an ancient Egyptian palace.

ADVANCED MATH

It was not until the 6th century A.D. that Arya-Bhata, a famous Hindu mathematician, had first worked out the first four decimal places of pi. Only 20 years before Taylor made his discovery, another English mathematician had reached a more accurate figure. But it seemed that the Egyptians had worked out the accurate decimal value of pi more than 4,000 years earlier!

"A wave of interest in ancient Egypt swept through Europe."

The Great Pyramid, surrounded by several smaller ones, in Egypt. Were these pyramids just burial sites, or did they have mysterious, otherworldly powers?

Taylor became convinced that the Great Pyramid recorded the size of the Earth and the length of the year. Further, he worked out that it had been built in around 2100 B.C. But this presented a problem. Biblical scholars claimed that the Great Flood as described in the Bible had happened in 2400 B.C. Taylor could not believe that, in just 300 years, the Egyptians had learned enough to make such mathematical observations.

DIVINE INSPIRATION

To Taylor, the answer was quite clear. It was divine inspiration that had ordered the building of Noah's Ark, to save humankind from the Flood. And it was divine inspiration that had ordered the building of the Great Pyramid, too.

Taylor was 78 years old when he announced the results of his findings. He died five years later, in 1864. However, he had made an important ally, or supporter. This ally was Charles Piazzi Smyth, who was the most respected astronomer in Scotland at the time. In 1864, Smyth went to Egypt to make his own measurements of the Great Pyramid. He confirmed Taylor's figures.

THE PYRAMIDOLOGISTS

Smyth was sure that his measurements had revealed all kinds of facts about the Earth and the universe, including the distance of Earth from the Sun. But other scientists laughed at him. They called him a "pyramidiot." As one American critic put it: "If a suitable unit of measurement is found, an exact equivalent to the distance to Timbuktu is certain to be found in the number of street lamps in Bond Street, or the . . . weight of adult goldfish!"

This is one of the tunnels inside the Great Pyramid. The pyramidologists claimed to have worked out when the world would end from the measurements of all the passages in the pyramid.

However, some people believed in the findings of Taylor and Smyth. They were convinced that the Great Pyramid, by Divine Inspiration, told the whole story of the human race. These believers took the measurements of the passages and chambers in the pyramid and used them to represent years, months, and days. Taking the date of creation as 4000 B.C., they predicted that the end of the world would come on the longest day of the year in A.D. 2045.

STRANGE COINCIDENCE

These believers became known as the "pyramidologists." One well-known pyramidologist was David Davidson, an engineer from Leeds, England. He published his findings in 1924. Among his measurements was the length of the passage between the Grand Gallery and the King's Chamber. He found that it could be converted to the period between August 4, 1914, and November 11, 1918—exactly the length of World War I.

". . . the end of the world would come on the longest day of the year in A.D. 2045."

For years, little was heard from the pyramidologists. But other strange facts related to the Great Pyramid sparked their interest once again. Werner von Siemens, the founder of the giant German electrical company, had paid a visit to the Great Pyramid in 1859. He climbed to the top, stood there like a conqueror, and pointed his finger into the air. He

A building on Angel Island, Mexico, is struck by lightning. A lightning rod fixed to the top is the only thing that saved this building from destruction.

received a mild electric shock. In itself, this is not too surprising. Nearly a century before this, Benjamin Franklin had shown that electricity could be given off from storm clouds. And all high buildings, such as church steeples and office blocks, have structures called "lightning rods" fixed to their tops so that they will not be damaged by lightning. The rod takes the electrical current safely to the ground.

OTHER POWERS

Meanwhile, in the 1920s Antoine Bovis, a French dealer in iron and hardware, had visited the Great Pyramid. He noticed the bodies of several cats and other animals that had crept into the King's Chamber and died there. They were dried out and mummified. When he got home to Nice, in France, Bovis decided to experiment. He built a wooden model of the pyramid and put a dead cat inside. It mummified in a few days. Next, he tried meat and eggs. In every case, instead of decaying they simply dried out.

This picture shows a man who claimed that these strange metal pyramids made his rhubarb grow quickly. He bought the pyramids from the army, but what they were used for remains a mystery.

In Czechoslovakia, a radio engineer named Karl Drbal heard about Bovis's experiments. He built a tiny pyramid of cardboard, only 6 inches (15 cm) high. Flowers and meat dried inside it, without decaying. Then Drbal put in a used razor blade, at a height one-third of the way up from the bottom— which related to the position of the King's Chamber in the real pyramid. Drbal claimed that it became sharp again. In 1959, after 10 years of pestering the Czech authorities, Drbal was allowed to market his Cheops Pyramid Razor Blade Sharpeners.

NEW AGE INTEREST

This began a new era of interest in the mysteries of the Great Pyramid. All over the world, people began to build model pyramids for themselves. They were used in meditation and for many sorts of healing purposes. At Glendale, in California, Patrick Flanagan decided to go into business. He sold pyramid tents, and "energy plates," made by joining several small pyramids. Remembering the experience of Werner von Siemens in 1859, Flanagan claimed that "biocosmic energy," which is electrical or other forms of energy, is concentrated in pyramid-shaped objects.

UNANSWERED QUESTIONS

Scientists at Stanford Research Institute decided to investigate. They did not get the same results as Bovis and Drbal. They reported that "eggs came out of our pyramid after 43 days, a smelly, runny yellow, and full of sediment. Tomatoes fared [lasted] no better than those in brown paper bags. We were unable to sharpen razor blades."

Another question for the pyramidologists has been: What happened to the Great Pyramid's pointed top? By the time people found the pyramid, it only had a flat top. Some have said that the point was made of gold and was stolen more than 1,000 years ago. When the Sun shone on it, this golden top would have concentrated the energy of the Sun's rays. And, shining brilliantly, it would have been visible far away. Perhaps, they suggest, the light was a signal to alien visitors from Space.

ANOTHER WORLD

The mystery of the Great Pyramid still fascinates archaeologists and pyramidologists alike. As William Fix put it, in his book *Pyramid Odyssey*: "It is enormous; it is ancient; it is legendary; it is sophisticated; it is the result of great enterprise [creative activity]; it is here, for all to see, at the crossroads of the Earth— and it does not seem to belong to our world."

The Search for Eldorado

Stories of a golden kingdom in the jungles of South America began a treasure hunt that has never ended.

In the 16th century, some Spanish explorers returned to Europe from South America with a wonderful tale. Somewhere deep in the heart of the continent, they had been told, stood an ancient city. Every year, there was a fantastic ceremony. The ruler of this city covered his body with gold dust. Then, he set out on a raft across a nearby lake. He plunged into the water to wash the dust away. At the end of the ceremony, his people threw gold and jewels into the lake as offerings to the gods. The Spaniards called the ruler of this ancient city El Dorado, meaning "the gilded one."

A GOLDEN CITY

In about 1530, a Spanish soldier was abandoned by his companions while they were exploring the Orinoco River in Venezuela. He said he was found by native peoples, who took him to a city that was hidden deep in the jungle. This was called Omagua, and it stood by a great lake. He said the roofs of the buildings were made of gold. There, he said, he met El Dorado.

The Spaniards were very excited by these tales of gold and jewels. Several expeditions set

Treasures such as this gold mask (opposite) are said to lie in the mud at the bottom of Lake Guatavita, in Colombia, South America.

40

"... his people threw gold and jewels into the lake as offerings to the gods."

out to try and find the city. They struggled across the Andes Mountains from Quito, in Ecuador. They took boats down the Amazon River in Brazil. They searched eastward, from Colombia. But they could find no trace of the "gilded one." Soon, the word "Eldorado" came to mean a whole fabulous kingdom. It was said that the ground was covered with gold. Although nobody knew exactly where Eldorado was, various locations were guessed at, and the places were marked on ancient maps.

Sir Walter Raleigh, whose failure to find the golden city of Eldorado resulted in his death.

RALEIGH FAILS

In 1595, an English sailor named Sir Walter Raleigh took boats to explore the waters of the Orinoco. He hoped to find Eldorado. He wanted to take gold back to England, where it was urgently needed to pay for the army and navy. On his return, Raleigh wrote a book that described "the golden city of Manoa (which the Spaniards call El Dorado)." But he did not take any gold back to England with him.

For political reasons, Raleigh was thrown into prison in 1603. In 1616, when he was already 62 years old, he promised that he would bring gold back from Eldorado if he was let out of prison. He was released and set off to search for Eldorado. But again he was unsuccessful. When he returned to England in 1618, he was executed.

As time passed, most people decided that Eldorado did not exist. It was just a myth. But the South American rain forests cover a huge area, and other lost cities have been found in similar places. However, even when it became possible to explore by airplane, the thick vegetation of the treetops hid everything. Then, in 1925, the English explorer Colonel Percy H. Fawcett decided to search once more.

A LOST CAUSE

While traveling in Brazil, Colonel Fawcett had come across a map. It was said to be over 150 years old and was drawn by a man who had found a lost city deep in the Mato Grosso region of southwest Brazil. The city was said to be surrounded by a wall.

Fawcett set off to find the city, taking his son Jack and a young friend named Raleigh Rimmel with him. Before he left, Fawcett wrote: "Whether we

A boy paddling his canoe in the Amazon rain forest. Over the centuries, many people have searched the jungle in the hope of finding the treasures of Eldorado.

succeed . . . and come out [of the jungle] alive, or whether we leave our bones there, of this I am certain: the key to the mystery of ancient South America, and perhaps of the whole of prehistory, can be found if we are able to locate these old cities."

"They reported that they had heard of another ruined city on the edge of a large lake."

"Their existence I do not for a moment doubt—how could I? I myself have seen a portion of one [city], and that is the reason why I observed it was imperative for me to go again. The remains seemed to be those of an outpost of one of the largest cities, which I am convinced is to be found, together with others, if a properly organized search is carried out. I have traveled through regions unknown to other explorers, and the . . . Indians have told me, time and again, of the buildings and the strange things to be found there."

FINAL MESSAGE

The last message from Fawcett's expedition came from deep in the jungle, at a place they named Dead Horse Camp. They reported that they had heard of another ruined city on the edge of a large lake. Then Fawcett and his two companions disappeared—never to be heard from again.

Some people believed that Fawcett had discovered the lost city and had decided to stay there. In 1936, a well-known psychic named Geraldine Cummins claimed to have received "spirit messages" from him. They said: "You must accept my assurance that the last relics of an ancient civilization, Egyptian in character, are to be found in central South America. With my living eyes I have seen those ruins."

MORE CLUES

In the meantime, however, the actual lake site of the ancient ceremony of El Dorado, as reported by the Spanish explorers in the 16th century, had been identified. This is Lake Guatavita, around 45 miles (72 km) northeast of the city of Bogotá, the capital of Colombia—and more than 2,000 miles (3,220 km) from where Fawcett disappeared. A small model, made from solid gold, was found in the waters of this lake. The model is of a raft. On it stands the figure of the great ruler El Dorado, attended by his priests.

This is the gold model of El Dorado that was found in the waters of Lake Guatavita. The model is now in a museum in Bogotá, Colombia.

Lake Guatavita is said to be the site of the ancient ceremony of El Dorado. Can its waters hold the key to the lost city of Omagua and the kingdom of Eldorado?

The legend of the gold and jewels that were thrown into the waters of the lake attracted many people to the site. For many years, people greedy for the gold tried to drain the lake. However, they were all unsuccessful. In the end, the Colombian government declared Lake Guatavita a protected national monument. They have forbidden any further attempts to empty its water or take its treasures.

WONDERS OF THE ANCIENT WORLD

There are no signs of the lost city of Omagua. The southern part of Colombia includes rivers that run into the Amazon. Beyond, in Brazil, stretches the unexplored vastness of the Mato Grosso. Perhaps, some day, a ruined city will be found there to rival the wonders of Tiahuanaco, the Toltec remains of Central America, or the great pyramids of Egypt.

Glossary

ancestor A member of the same family from a previous generation.

archaeologist A person who studies the history of the art and dwellings of past human life.

ascending Climbing or rising upward from the ground.

assurance A promise or guarantee that something is true.

astronomer A person who studies the stars and planets.

astronomy The scientific study of the stars and planets.

expedition A trip or journey to find out about something.

extinct No longer alive or active.

granite A very hard gray or red rock often used for building.

horizontal Parallel to the horizon.

latitude A distance north or south of the equator, which is measured in degrees.

longitude A distance measured in degrees east or west of an imaginary line that passes from north to south through Greenwich, in England.

meditation Time spent in deep thought, while the body is relaxed.

mummified Something preserved due to the removal of all fluids.

observatory A place where scientists study the planets and stars, or other natural objects such as animals and birds.

pharaoh A king of ancient Egypt.

philosopher Someone who studies the nature and meaning of life.

prehistory Before humans began to keep written historical records.

primitive The earliest stages of human history, or something that is simple or basic.

psychic A person who claims to be able to see into the future, or who has other unexplained powers.

rain forest A dense growth of trees over a large area in the tropics. The treetops form a "roof" that is home to many animals and birds.

relic Something old from the past, such as a small statue or ancient ruin. Also, objects that are said to be holy.

thatch A roof covering made from straw and reeds.

vegetation All the plants that are found growing together in one particular place.

vertical Upright, or at right angles to the horizon.

volcanic Something produced by, or caused by, a volcano. For example, volcanic rock.

Index

Further Reading

Barber, Nicola. *The Search for Gold*, "Treasure Hunters" series. Raintree Steck-Vaughn, 1998

Clark, Lynette and Clark, Dexter. *On Golden Ground: Our Journey to the Eldorado*. Larson and Larrigan, 1997

Ganeri, Anita. *The Search for Tombs*, "Treasure Hunters" series. Raintree Steck-Vaughn, 1998

Martell, Hazel M. *The Great Pyramid*, "Great Buildings" series. Raintree Steck-Vaughn, 1998